949

GW01005416

A Family in t
1920s
Valerie Fawcett

**Katy finds
out about her
great grandparents**

Oxford University Press 1993

What was life like in the 1920s?
This is where Katy's great grandparents lived then.
They were called Ada and Thomas.
They had a baby called Jean in 1920.

Ada did not go into hospital to have the baby.
A midwife came to the house to help with the birth.
They put warm clothes on Jean.
Houses did not have central heating then.
There was a coal fire in each room.

Most people at that time did not have a bathroom.
If Ada and Thomas wanted a bath, they heated
water on the range.
Then they filled a big tin bath in the kitchen.

Afterwards, they poured the water down the drain outside.

The toilet was outside the back door, in a little shed.

5

6

Ada worked at home, looking after the children.
There were no washing machines, so Ada scrubbed
the clothes with a bar of soap on a washboard.
Then she put them through a mangle to squeeze the
water out.
Ada had to put her iron on the range to make it hot.
There were no electric irons.

Every day, the baker came round in a van to sell bread.
A horse pulled the van.
The milkman came round too.
When Jean was 5, she went to get the milk.
She took a jug out to the cart and the milkman filled it up.

8

Sometimes the muffin man came along the
street at teatime.
He rang his bell to tell people he was there.
Jean loved muffins with jam.

The lamplighter came round to light the street lamps.
He used a long pole to switch on and light each lamp.
The lamps were not electric. They were gas.
The lights inside the house were gas lamps as well.
Ada lit the lamps with a taper.

10

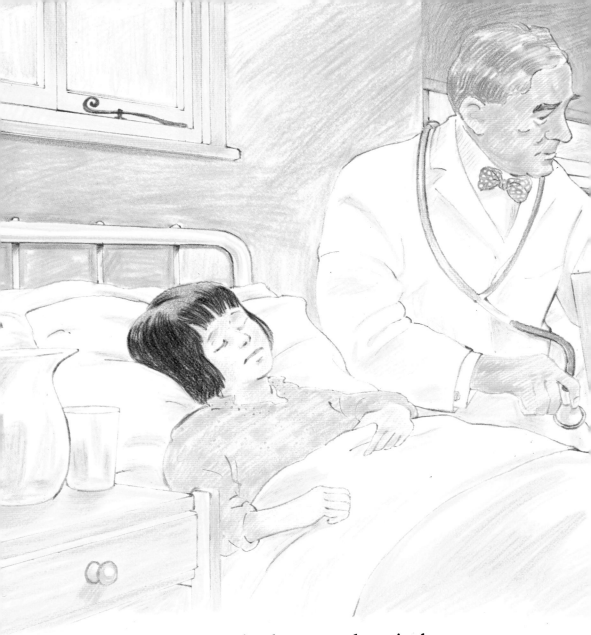

When she was 7, Jean had to go to hospital.
She had an illness called scarlet fever and she was very ill.
Jean's mum and dad were not allowed to visit her.

At that time, people had some illnesses which we do
not have today.
They did not have the medicines they needed to get well.
Jean got better but a lot of children died.

When Jean was better, Ada and Thomas took her and
her brother to the cinema for a treat.
The film was black and white and there was no sound.
You had to read the words.

14

A woman played the piano while people watched the film.
When the story was sad, she played slow music.
When there was a chase, she played very fast music.

Jean could not watch television.
There were no televisions when Jean was a little girl.

Ada and Thomas had one of the first radios.
It was called a crystal set.
You had to wear headphones to hear the programme.
Sometimes it was very difficult to hear.

There were 50 children in Jean's class at school.
They learnt to read and write and do sums and they
practised handwriting a lot.
The boys also made things with wood and the girls
learnt to sew.

If they did something wrong, the teacher hit them with a cane.
The girls and boys did not play together.
They had separate playgrounds.

19

In 1928 the family went to the seaside for a holiday.
First, they went on a tram to the station.
Trams were like buses but they ran on rails in the road.
Then the family got on a train.

The train was a steam train which meant that there was a coal fire in the engine.

This fire heated water to make steam, and the power of the steam made the engine work.

Jean liked the train ride as much as the holiday.

Katy's Family Tree

Ada, born in 1890
Katy's Great Gran

Thomas, born in 1890
Katy's Great Grandad

married in 1918

Charles,
born in 1919

Jean,
born in 1920
Katy's Gran

Irene,
born in 1921

Dorothy,
born in 1923

Will,
born in 1930

George, born in 1919, **Katy's** Grandad

married in 1946

Martin, born in 1953
Katy's Dad

Susan, born in 1953
Katy's Mum

John, born in 1946
Katy's Uncle

married
in 1975

Katy, born in 1986

Tom, born in 1978

Prices

d = old penny   s = shilling

4d (1¾p)

4½d (2p)

1s 1d (5½p)

£300

£20

No televisions to buy

How much did people earn each week?

Engine driver £4 10s (£4.50)

Factory worker £3 4s 10d (£3.24p)

Index

Acknowledgements
Illustrations: Barry Rowe (main pictures and cover),
and Lynne Willey (family tree, title page and back cover).
Photos: Rob Judges

Oxford University Press, Walton Street,
Oxford, OX2 6DP
© Oxford University Press 1993
ISBN 0 19 917174 2
Phototypeset by Pentacor, High Wycombe, Bucks
Printed in Hong Kong